DANCES OF ARGENTINA

General Editor

W. O. GALBRAITH

Technical Editor

JOAN WILDEBLOOD

Plate 1 *El Bailecito.*   (*Figure 1, Vuelta General*)

Dances of
ARGENTINA

A. L. LLOYD

PUBLISHED
UNDER THE AUSPICES OF
THE ROYAL ACADEMY OF DANCING
AND THE
LING PHYSICAL EDUCATION
ASSOCIATION

MAX PARRISH·LONDON

Contents

Music arranged by Jorge Arturo Mora

Illustrations by Lucile Armstrong

PRINTED IN GREAT BRITAIN BY
BILLING AND SONS LTD GUILDFORD
MUSIC PHOTO-SET BY
HALSTAN AND CO LTD AMERSHAM

Introduction

The most important single factor in the creation of the Argentine folk-dance was the presence of the gaucho, the rough cattle-man of the plains. The Spanish *conquistadores* had civilised the mountain country of the north, but they did not push far south on to the vast plains, among the high grasses of the pampa. The civilisers of the pampa were the gauchos, with their baggy trousers, their immense spurs, their broad belts decorated with silver coins. In the popular imagination, the gaucho – like the Texas cowboy – means sweat, swagger, and sudden death. He also means poetry, music, and dance of a special vernacular kind. In general, the folk-culture of northern Argentina is shared by Chile, Peru, Bolivia. But the folk-culture of the pampa is Argentina's own exclusive property.

To understand the dances of the gaucho, it is necessary to understand the man himself. The desperate loneliness of the pampa, the endless struggle with rigorous Nature, spirited cattle, and hostile Indians, created a character quite unlike the peasant, the normal bearer of folk-culture. In manners, techniques, dress, often in blood too, the old-time gaucho had as much of the Indian as of the Spaniard. He was tough, cruel, restless, barbarous, a man who habitually ate from his hands with neither plate nor bowl, whose wealth was his horse, and whose argument was the *facón*, a knife as long as a bayonet.

The gaucho has been called a beggar on horseback, and so he was. His was a civilisation of the horse. A man afoot was an orphan. The gaucho churned his butter by dragging a hide bag of milk across the plain at a gallop. He cured his meat by laying it between the saddle and the horse's back before a long ride. Some of his dances contain steps that imitate the pawing of a stallion. In others, the spurs are used as a musical instrument. Poverty and rootlessness he wore as a badge of independence; but with what an air! If he imitated the Indian in the shifts which would give him mastery over his surroundings, he drew from his Spanish ancestors his sense of courtesy, gravity and elegance. It is these characteristics, combined with the Indian's sinewy toughness, which are the most remarkable feature of the gaucho dances.

Rare was the gaucho who could not extract some kind of music from the guitar, and one of the most celebrated national types was the *payador*, the gaucho minstrel, respected and fêted wherever he went, living by his capacity to improvise songs and dance tunes, with a bunch of pink and blue streamers hanging from the head of his guitar, recalling the girls who had favoured him with the ribbons from their hair.

This was the type of man who played an important part in the fight for Argentina's independence from Spain. And when independence was won, the gauchos made up the private armies of the cattle-owning *caudillos* in the long-drawn war for supremacy between the nationalist conservatism of the countryside and the cosmopolitan liberalism of the towns. This, in a land where the sense of nationalism is strong, has made the gaucho a revered symbol, and versions of gaucho ways, gaucho costume, gaucho dances, are to be encountered, in varying degrees of authenticity, not only in the countryside, but even in the heart of Buenos Aires itself.

However, the gaucho's 'national' form of folklore is not the only folklore Argentina has. Other forces were also at work. Much of gaucho culture was a hybrid comprised of elements drawn from the later Spanish colonisers and the savage Indians of the plains; but in the north-west, towards the Andes, folk-culture was of a more refined, more ancient order, a hybrid of early Spanish models and the well-developed native culture of the Inca empire. As we have seen, whereas the folk-dances of the plains (the *chacareras, gatos, escondidos*, etc.) may be considered strictly Argentine, those of the northern mountains (the *carnavalitos, bailecitos, cuecas*, etc.) are shared with Argentina's neighbours. The mountain folk-culture, more archaic but at the same time more durable than that of the plains, has been a constant fertilising influence, though sometimes the enthusiasts forget the enormous debt that is owed to those stolid mountaineers, poor and ragged men whose features often evoke the warriors in bright feathered cloaks, with silver swords, who marched in the armies of the great Inca Atahualpa.

These, then, are the two main sources of Argentine folk-dance – the old-European and Inca hybrid of the Andean mountains, and the newer-European and native hybrid of the plains.

The Growth of the Dances

What is a folk-dance? The scholars cannot agree. Some, with the strictest view, would limit the term to those dances deriving from ancient ceremony (round dances and chain dances), without any trace of urban influence. Of this kind, few examples survive in Argentina, though the figured round-dance known in the north-west as the *carnavalito*, and the maypole dance – also north-western – called the *danza de las cintas* show their ceremonial origin quite clearly. In general, it appears that the dances of rural Argentina derive, with varying degrees of adaptation, from the aristocratic ballroom dances of Europe, and particularly of Paris (though it is worth noting that often these ballroom dances have themselves evolved from earlier folk models).

Some enthusiasts bitterly oppose the notion that their national dances have a foreign origin. They prefer to believe that the *criollo* (native) dances of Argentina are the spontaneous invention of the gaucho, or are derived from

7

Spanish folk-dances, or else are a formalisation of aboriginal Indian dances. But in fact, neither in the primitive culture of the pampa Indians nor in the higher culture of the former inhabitants of the Inca empire are couple-dances known, whereas the strictly criollo dances are for couples, with the exception of the *malambo*, a showy solo dance of putative Negro origin. And though the texts of some of the dance-songs derive from Spanish models, there are no clear traces of Spanish folk-style in the criollo dances (nor in criollo costume, nor in the folk-instruments; and very little in the folk-music itself). As for the gaucho spontaneously creating his own dances, it is true that the cattle-hand set the imprint of his rough thumb on the choreography of the countryside; but his role was that of the inspired adapter rather than the creator.

Carlos Vega, whose work in the investigation of Argentine folk-music and -dance may be compared to that of Cecil Sharp in England, has traced* the path by which a dance may arrive in the yard of a tumbledown shack where the gauchos have hung up their ropes and branding-irons and the girls have set down their water-buckets. The new dance may have been learned from the surrounding rural population, who picked it up from the nearest country town. It arrived in the small-town dance-hall from the provincial capital, having been brought there, perhaps, by fashionable travellers from the metropolis. It would probably be carried to that metropolis by even more fashionable travellers from some foreign capital – from Paris, Vienna, or more recently New York.

So a dance may have made its long journey from, say, the ballrooms of Versailles to the cattle-yards of Huachipampa. It may have taken generations to arrive, and by the time it reached the back blocks, its appearance would have so changed that the dancing-master who created it would fail

*In ORIGEN DE LOS BAILES CRIOLLOS (*Comisión Nacional de Cultura: Conferencias del ciclo 1941: Buenos Aires*).

to recognise his own child. It should be remarked that the transformation of the aristocratic ballroom dance into the sinewy picaresque dance of the plains did not proceed at an even rate. While the dances remained in the cities, they would doubtless be relatively little changed, but once they spread into the countryside they would immediately be subject to the working of the creative imagination of the unlettered folk, who would improvise on the existing patterns, adapting the dances to suit their psychological needs and preferences, and thus create new dances, loosely called 'traditional'.

From the Conquest to the beginning of the nineteenth century, the infiltration of European dances into the Argentine provinces was by way of Lima. After 1810, Buenos Aires became the centre of diffusion. But the newer dances coming in by way of Buenos Aires never showed the powers of adaptation, the capacity for developing new species, which had marked the dances diffused from Lima. Whereas the old galliards and courantes had undergone drastic transformation into such 'folk' dances as the *gato* and the *zamacueca*, the minuets and gavottes of the late eighteenth century were only lightly modified into Argentine 'native' ballroom dances, such as the *federal* or the *cuando*. And the dances that followed, from the polka to the fox-trot, reached the Argentine countryside almost entirely unchanged.

As Curt Sachs emphasised in his 'World History of the Dance', history has seen three great cycles of dance: collective dance, individual dance, dance for couples.

The characteristic criollo dances are dances for couples, but for couples whose partners are separate from each other, and not embracing in the modern ballroom style of, for example, the waltz. Among these dances for detached couples, Carlos Vega distinguishes two groups: the 'picaresque' dances for one independent couple, such as the *chacarera* and the *escondido* (though occasionally, through outside influences, these dances came to admit formations

9

of four or more dancers, as was the case with the *bailecito*); and the 'serious' dances for various couples, such as the *cielito* and the *pericón*, in which the movements of all the couples are co-ordinated to achieve each figure of the dance.

The first dances for embraced couples – the waltz, polka, mazurka, schottische – reached the plains towards the middle of the nineteenth century. With their arrival began the decline of the brilliant criollo choreography of former times. The authentic folk-dance areas of Argentina shrank rapidly. By the nineteen-twenties the once widely-popular national dances of Argentina, both 'picaresque' and 'serious', were flourishing in their natural state only in the remoter reaches of the north, from Santiago del Estero to the Bolivian frontier. Incidentally, the Argentine tango, essentially a creation of the metropolis, first appeared on the scene in May 1907, though the Andalusian *tango flamenco* had reached Argentina, as a stage and circus dance, in the eighteen-eighties.

In recent times, the urban populations of Argentina have begun to take a keen interest in the folk-dances of their country. Folk-dances are much taught in schools, and are a favourite stage spectacle in many city cafés. Among young folk, criollo dancing enjoys a vogue similar to that of square-dancing in the United States and Britain, and is often attended by similar deformations and eccentricities. This vogue is effecting something of a revival of criollo dancing in country districts too, and many folk-dances which were on the point of withering away have come back into blossom.

El Carnavalito

The aboriginal peoples of Argentina have a number of primitive dances of their own, but in general these have had little influence on what one must call the folk-dances of the country. A possible exception is the carnavalito. This is a modern version of those collective round dances which have persisted since primitive time, and whose most spectacular European forms are the Balkan *hora* (variously known as *kolo*, *horo*, etc.).

In north-western Argentina, the carnavalito is danced by all social classes. The Indians have it in its most primitive form; among the poorer rural population it is more evolved, but still simple, with just two or three figures; and in the dance-halls and ballrooms of the Andean towns, the carnavalito exists in highly complex form, enriched with elements drawn from the cultured dances of Europe. It is arguable whether the carnavalito should be considered a European importation rather than an aboriginal derivative.

It is in the mountain areas of Jujuy and Salta that the carnavalito exists in its liveliest, most vigorous form. At fiesta times, Christian, pagan, or political, as you approach a settlement in, say, the Humahuaca Canyon beloved of folklorists, you might hear the thumpity-thump of the small drums coming to you along the ravine. As you get nearer, you might distinguish the shrill note of the Indian flute and the jangle of the ukulele-like *charangos*. And there, perhaps in front of a little white-washed church, a circle of blanketed men and women – some with babies on their backs – are dancing round the standing musicians.

Some of the dancers may wave a corn-cob or a sprig of sweet basil, though they would find it hard to give a reason, for the harvest-magical significance has been forgotten. Round they go, then, switching the changes on a few simple figures, the wheel, the double wheel, the chain. The leader carries a handkerchief or a ribboned stick, and sometimes he calls the changes in a high hoarse voice. In this form, the carnavalito may last for hours, just as it does in its aboriginal form.

The fullest development of the dance, with the most elaborate and ingenious formations, is found among the North-Argentine townsfolk. This 'social' version of the old round, which is also popular in Bolivia, seems to have

Plate 2 El Carnavalito.   (Figure 2, Las Alas)

spread from the colonial salons of High Peru. The form in which the dance appears in this volume is mid-way between its simplest folk-form and its complex ballroom form.

La Chacarera

The chacarera is one of the best-loved of criollo dances. Indeed, it is one of the few that still persist as survivals and not merely as revivals, and it preserves some of the most archaic characters to be found in criollo dancing. At present, its authentic performance is limited to lower-class gatherings in the north, but fifty years ago it was danced in all Argentine provinces except Patagonia, and was a particular favourite of the gauchos of the pampa. Thanks to the efforts of folklorists, teachers and professional artistes, the chacarera is beginning to spread again.

The history of the chacarera is obscure, and references to it in the literature of the past are so scanty that some scholars believe the dance must have had some other name until the mid-nineteenth century. The chacarera belongs to that extensive group of picaresque dances deriving from old-European forms, and diffused during colonial times from Lima to many parts of the South American continent. As often happens with dances among rural populations, the performance of the chacarera differed from region to region. The foundation of the dance remained the same, but each province had its own idiomatic style. The version given here is the one of widest diffusion, at once the simplest and most characteristic form of the dance.

El Escondido

The escondido is a true folk-dance whose popularity spread to the cultured classes early in the nineteenth century, when the movement for national independence had promoted a wide interest in the vernacular arts of the gaucho. Besides its picaresque liveliness, it is also remarkable for the pantomimic episode of the 'lost partner': at certain moments in the dance, one partner hides – merely symbolically, by sinking on one knee and covering the eyes – while the other gyrates as if making a search.

This choreographic element, which has, at first sight, an artificial appearance, is of a type occasionally encountered in folk-dances in many parts of the world. In the escondido, it may be a modern interpolation, or it may be of ancient origin, deriving from some dance-drama or dance-game.

Like many other criollo dances, the escondido was known in all provinces fifty years ago, and was considered as a gaucho dance. Nowadays it survives authentically only among the – mainly non-gaucho – rural population of the north-west. However, perhaps on account of its attractive element of pantomime, it is a favourite of the city-inspired folk-dance revival.

El Bailecito

This graceful handkerchief dance, whose full name – rarely used – is *bailecito de tierra*, has a wider dissemination in Peru and Bolivia than in Argentina, where it was always traditionally confined to the northern provinces of Salta and Jujuy, and, perhaps through stage performances, to Tucumán, Catamarca, and Santiago del Estero. However, the form which the bailecito acquired in Jujuy has such special characteristics that it must be considered as an Argentine folk-dance.

Like other criollo dances, the bailecito has been produced by the action of generations of South American dancers, particularly in rural areas, working over and adapting certain fashionable old-time court and ballroom dances from Europe (which themselves had a rustic origin, as often as not).

Argentine folk-dances, particularly the older, more rural, picaresque type, are usually for one couple only. No doubt, the bailecito was originally of this kind. But perhaps through the influence of French set dances, such as the quadrilles, in the nineteenth century, the Argentine bailecito has become a kind of square for four or more dancers, though considerably less 'rectilinear' than the French ballroom squares.

The documentation of the bailecito is scanty and imprecise, perhaps because the term was once applied indiscriminately to all kinds of picaresque dances. The first description of its choreography was published in 'La Prensa' in 1933. Since then, it has become a particularly well-loved dance among middle-class enthusiasts, both in the cities and the smaller provincial towns. Among the lower classes, it is rarely seen outside its 'home country', the folkloristically rich areas of Jujuy and northern Salta.

Music

Argentine folk-music consists in the main of a mixture of Spanish popular music* and the music of the aboriginal Indians. These two elements are present in varying degrees of intensity. Roughly, the farther north one goes from Buenos Aires, and the older the musical type, the more Indian characteristics one is likely to find in the music.

In the relatively modern music of the pampa country, the European idiom predominates, and there is little trace of aboriginal musical influence. The music of the Araucanians of the south seems to have had little power to mingle with European-style music. In that respect it is very different from the music of the northern Indians, which has shown great capacity for assimilation. Consequently, where Indian influences are met with in Argentine folk-music, they are usually Quichua (in the north-west) or Guarany (in the north-east). The Guarany-influenced music of those provinces abutting on Paraguay and Brazil is on the whole of a rather superficial kind, possessing more charm than vigour, well-suited for performance by small light-music ensembles

*The term 'popular' music is used here advisedly; the Spanish influence on Argentine dance-tunes comes rather more from humble stage and circus music than from the folk-music proper of the Iberian Peninsula.

in cafés and hotels. The Quichua-influenced music of the Andean country is certainly the richest, liveliest and most profound of all types of Argentine folk-music.

The Quichua were the dominant peoples in the old Inca empire, and their musical culture was high before the arrival of the *conquistadores*. Their music quickly became subject to the influences of Spanish music, and not of folk-music merely. The priests who came with the colonisers had the double task of converting the Indians and educating the young Spaniards. In their curriculum, music played a special part, because of the native gifts of both Spaniards and Indians.

If, in the upper reaches of society, music remained predominantly classical and European, among the lower classes the native Indian styles mingled happily with Spanish popular music to create that bright hybrid that is still to be heard in the dance-halls and village-squares of the north. Characteristic of much of this music is the use of pentatonic scales, of binary rhythms and of parallel thirds in singing and instrumental playing. Also a number of tritonic tunes, usually based on the scale of (*do*) *fa la do*, are to be found among these hybrids of the north-western mountain regions.

The music of the plains, the gaucho music proper, contains little sign of Indian influence, being mainly a mixture of old Spanish colonial music and elements of more modern European popular styles, brought in during the nineteenth century along with the waltz, the mazurka, the schottische. The scale is usually the common European major, the harmonies are entirely European, the rhythms are predominantly ternary (but distinctive; it is chiefly in the rhythms that criollo music differs from the music of Western Europe).

Some pampa dance-tunes may contain elements deriving from Negro music. Negroes, now relatively rare in Argentina, were once numerous on the plains, as nineteenth-century pampa literature testifies. However, the role of the Negro in Argentine music has proved not easy to determine.

Instruments

The guitar is used to accompany folk-dancing and -singing all over the Republic. In the mountainous north, dancing may be supported by the voice – solo, in unison, or in parallel thirds – also by the *quena, charango, caja*, and *bombo*. On the pampa, besides guitar and voice, violin, accordion and bombo are often used to accompany the dances.

The guitar came to America as a salon instrument, not a folk-instrument. To this day it has remained primarily an urban, rather than a rural, instrument. In this respect it resembles the violin and the accordion, which are much played by folk-musicians, but cannot be classed as folk-instruments themselves. It seems to have been widely used in South America since 1600, first in a five-stringed form, later with six strings. For dance-music, it is generally strummed, but for accompanying songs, particularly of the older type, it is sometimes picked, parallel to the melody, a third lower than the voice.

The *quena*, the six-holed pipe, is the most famous of aboriginal American instruments. The pre-Hispanic Incas had quenas of bone, stone, and pottery. Now they are usually of cane. Much quena music is pentatonic, though the instrument itself has a scale resembling the European diatonic major. Over the last few years, perhaps with the increased influx of quena-playing Bolivian Indians, who cross the frontier in search of higher wages, the quena has been enjoying an enormous vogue.

The *charango* is a small guitar-shaped instrument with double-strings and a curved back like a mandoline. The frame is usually made from the carapace of an armadillo, soaked in hot water and squeezed into a mould. The instrument appears to date from the eighteenth century. It was originally gut-strung, but now the strings are usually of metal. The charango is held like a ukulele, and generally strummed, though some village performers have great skill in playing melody-style (picking) as well as rhythm-style.

The *bombo* resembles the modern European bass-drum, though sometimes made from local materials, with an oil-drum or hollow-trunk frame, for instance, instead of the bronze frame common in the cities. Bombos are sometimes classified as being of one-, two-, or three-leagues, according to the distance at which they can be heard. Bombo-players in country dance-bands usually play seated, with the instrument lying across their knees, right arm free, left arm on the frame, beating with a padded stick in one hand and an unpadded stick in the other, always on the right-hand parchment of the drum.

The *caja* is a flat drum, apparently of aboriginal origin, about five inches deep and thirteen inches across, with two membranes. The frame is usually of Bolivian wood, the parchment of sheepskin or dogskin, kept tense by a zigzag of rawhide thongs. The drum is held dangling from the left thumb by a leather loop. It may be played with two sticks or one, padded or unpadded, with blows alternating on the parchment and on the wooden frame.

Of the dances illustrated in this book, the carnavalito and bailecito would best be danced to *quena* (or recorder), guitar and small drum; the pampa dances, chacarera and escondido, would be best suited to a combination of guitar, violin (or accordion) and big drum.

The harp, clarinet, and triangle are also met with in Argentine folk-orchestras. It is noteworthy that Spanish folk-instruments, such as the castanets and *gaita* (bagpipes), are not found among Argentine folk-musicians.

Costume

In Argentina, the wearing of distinctively national costume is rather a man's affair than a woman's. Argentine costume does not show those regional differences sometimes encountered in Europe, where style, cut, and embellishment may vary from village to village. Argentina has two kinds of dress differing from ordinary European-style town clothes – the dress of the gauchos of the plains, and of the rural populations of the mountainous north.

Gaucho costume is determined by the needs and the showy fancies of the horse-riding cattlemen. Andean costume is basically the costume of humble men who herd sheep on foot. The two styles have one important garment in common – the *poncho*.

The poncho is a square blanket-like cloak, usually of wool, with an opening in the centre for the head to go through. It serves as a protection against weather, as a covering at night, and, wrapped round the forearm, as a shield in knife-fights.

Vicuña-wool ponchos are the lightest and most luxurious. They are also the most expensive, costing as much as £40. The common sheep's-wool *poncho puyo* is dyed in various colours – frequently blue with red stripes near the edge. The *poncho pampa* is a more spectacular garment, woven with rectangular Indian designs based on the motif of the cross. The colours of the poncho pampa are frequently the natural colours of the wool, black and white.

After the poncho, perhaps the most distinctive garment of the gaucho was the *chiripá*. It consisted of a wide strip of coarse cloth, usually flannel, passed loosely between the legs, and tucked under the sash, back and front. The chiripá, usually of beige with a black or brown stripe, was worn over cotton drawers. It was frequently of Scottish manufacture.

The chiripá was worn with *botas de potro*, soft rawhide boots made by cutting round the skin of a horse's leg well above the knee, and again just above the fetlock. The 'tube' of skin was then pulled off entire, well-kneaded to render it supple, and pulled on over the gaucho's foot and half-way up his leg, so that the man's heel was where the horse's knee had been. Toes were sometimes left free, and the tops of boots secured by a strip of embroidered material tied as a garter.

Nowadays, chiripás and botas de potro are no longer seen, except occasionally on the stage. The modern gaucho wears *bombachas* tucked into short-legged riding boots reaching half-way up the calf, sometimes with close concertina-folds about the ankle. Bombachas are wide-legged trousers buttoned at the ankle by a narrow band. They appear to have been of Balkan manufacture originally, though they are not worn in Balkan countries. They are usually black or navy-blue, sometimes brown.

With his bombachas, the gaucho wears a plain shirt, white, rose-coloured or blue, a short dark jacket, a kerchief, usually white, and a felt hat, usually black, with pork-pie style crown and a narrow brim turned up in the front and at the back. He wears a broad sash, pulled very tight, and over it a wide leather belt, heavily decorated with huge silver coins and held by an enormous circular fastening of silver, called a *rastra*. His spurs, too, are often enormous and elegant, and fine spurs and rastras are much sought-after by city collectors and antique-dealers.

After the gaucho costume, the costume of the Andean villages of the north seems very tame. Before the Conquest, the natives of the area dressed in colourful garments, and decorated their costume with gold and jewels and the bright plumage of birds. Now, centuries of poverty and suffering have affected their style of dress far more than, for example, their style of music.

Beside the poncho, the men wear a broad-brimmed low-crowned felt hat (the crown undented, as a rule), a cotton shirt, unbleached cotton trousers, and *ushutas*, or sandals, usually of rawhide or grass. Once, ushutas were made of vicuña wool, sewn and embroidered with gold thread. Of late, the rustics of northern Argentina have taken to making them of pieces of tyre-rubber, which wears better than raw-hide, and does not soften in water.

Nowadays, women all over Argentina prefer to wear everyday European clothes, but particularly in northern villages one still sees the old-fashioned calico dresses – a full skirt reaching to the ankles and beyond, usually without flounces; and a long-sleeved blouse with a frilled waist hanging outside the skirt. Country women wear the poncho in the north but not elsewhere. Their hair sometimes hangs down in braids; and, again in the north, the women often wear a man's broad-brimmed hat over a kerchief knotted beneath the chin. 'Revival' folk-dancers in the towns commonly wear long full skirts and short frilly blouses with short puffed sleeves, of spotted material as often as not, not because these clothes are 'authentic' but because they give a uniform appearance with some air of rusticity.

The Dances

Abbreviations used in description of steps and dances

r – right ⎱ referring to
l – left ⎰ hand, foot, etc.
C – clockwise

R – right ⎱ describing turns or
L – left ⎰ ground pattern
C-C – counter-clockwise

Poise of the Body, and Characteristic Arm Gestures

Most of the true Argentine criollo dances are for two dancers (man and woman) only. As a rule, the partners never touch.

The poise is dignified and upright, the head well-carried, the arms slightly bent so that the hands are held just a little higher and wider than the shoulders.

The movements are swift, graceful, vigorous, but never abrupt. The dances are grave, not showy. The woman's movements are quieter than the man's. Some gaucho dances contain passages for step-dancing (*zapateo*) for the male partner only. Many are accompanied with a light finger-snapping by both partners. These zapateos are often improvisations of high brilliance and virtuosity, but they require considerable practice.

These remarks do not, in general, apply to the Carnavalito, which is a collective round of different character from most criollo dances.

Basic Step

The basic step of nearly all criollo dances is the *caminado-valseado*, the 'waltzed walk' – one pace forward with the left foot, half a pace with the right, half a pace with the left, and the same again starting with the right foot. The motions are gliding, not springing.

The dance directions which follow are based largely on the authoritative instructions contained in Carlos Vega's *Las Danzas Populares Argentinas* (1952).

El Carnavalito

Region	The extreme north, particularly the provinces of Jujuy and Salta.
Character	Quick, light, gay.
Formation	Round dance for as many as will. In its most sophisticated forms, this dance may have as many as fifteen or twenty Figures. These may come in any order. The form given here comprises only those Figures which seem to have remained constant since the mid-eighteenth century. The changes are called by the dance-leader. (——=man, – – – =woman.)
The Step	Throughout, the dance is a 'jog-trot' run, the knees slightly lifted. Each step takes one beat.
Hand Clapping	(Figure 2) The elbows are kept in to sides, the fore-arms raised so that the palm of l hand is facing, and in a line with, the chest. The r hand is clapped into l hand.
Expression	Cheerful; smiling.

Musical Bars	The number of musical bars used by these Figures depends on the number of couples and thus the size of the circle. With fifteen or sixteen couples participating, it is usually easy to fit the Figures to the alternate 14- and 16-bar sections of the melody.

Dance

FIGURE 1: EL CIRCULO (THE CIRCLE)

The dancers in couples; each woman puts her l arm through her partner's r arm. They run in circle C, men on outside.

FIGURE 2: LAS ALAS (THE WINGS)

CENTRE BACK

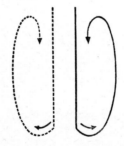

From centre-back, the lead couple advance down the middle. The others follow. On reaching the front, the couples separate, women to R, men to L; the two files each make a semi-circle and partners rejoin at centre-back. From the moment they separate till they rejoin, the dancers clap.

FIGURE 3: EL PUENTE (THE BRIDGE)

As the couples rejoin, the man takes the woman's l hand in his r, holding the hands forward, about the height of the elbow, as though guiding her firmly ahead, and the chain advances straight down the middle again. Reaching

CARNAVALITO (Cholita Traidora)

Arranged by J. A. MORA

D.C.

centre-front, the lead couple let go hands, and, making a half turn inwards towards each other, they lean forward to dance back under the raised arms of the other couples, who lift their clasped hands, man's r, woman's l. The lead woman gives her r arm to partner, who puts his l arm through hers. They dance under the 'bridge' to the last couple, and when they arrive there, the second couple follow, till the last couple have turned under their own 'bridge'. As each couple emerges from the 'bridge' they move round in a circle C, as in Figure 1, but this time the circle is much narrower, with the women on the outside.

FIGURE 4: EL MOLINO (THE MILL)
When the last couple from the 'bridge' have closed the circle, the women, letting go their partners, make a three-quarter turn outwards to their L, join hands in a ring outside the men, and dance in the contrary (C-C) direction. Meanwhile, the men join hands in an inner ring and continue in their former direction. The two circles continue in counter motion for one complete turn, till they arrive at their own partners, when the men break into the circle of women as follows in the next Figure.

FIGURE 5: LA RUEDA (THE WHEEL)
In breaking the women's circle, each man takes his partner's l arm through his r arm, and she gives her r arm to the l arm of man on her R. Thus all dancers with linked arms proceed C in a large circle, making one complete turn, to arrive back where the Figure began.

FIGURE 6: LAS VOLTERETAS (THE WHIRLIGIGS)
As soon as the lead couple have reached centre-back, each man releases his own partner. The woman on his l arm continues running forward but is swung round him, while the man runs on the spot, as if marking time, turning round (backwards) to his R, both going round once. Then

the whole circle continues round as before, with linked arms, but each time the lead couple reach one of the four cardinal points, marked X, of the circle all do this same *voltereta* until finally they are back at their starting point.

CENTRE BACK

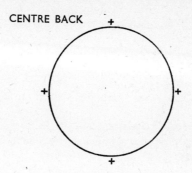

FIGURE 7: EL CARACÓL (THE SNAIL)

During the last *voltereta*, each couple unlink arms and join hands. As the circle re-forms, each woman gives her free hand to the man behind her, but the leader does not take the hand of the last woman in the chain. Instead, he deviates a little from his path and leads the file about a yard in towards the centre. The others following, the chain begins to coil in on itself like a snail-shell. Then, before it coils too tight, the leader shouts and turning round to his L, he leads the line back until the spiral has uncoiled.

FIGURE 8: EL CÍRCULO (THE CIRCLE)

When the chain has uncoiled, and the leader finds himself once more at the centre-back, he makes a left-hand turn, swinging his (own) right-hand partner (who must release the l hand of the man behind her) round with him, to reverse their direction, to go round C. As each couple arrives at the centre-back they do the same, until all the dancers are back again as in Figure 1.

La Chacarera

Region	Once common all over Argentina, except Patagonia. Much danced on the pampa. Now found chiefly from Santiago del Estero northwards.
Character	A graceful, dignified though picaresque dance.
Formation	For one independent couple only.
Step	A flat, level waltz step, one waltz step to each bar of 6/8 time. The size of the steps varies according to the Figure.
Arm Position	Rather square. Upper arm almost to shoulder level, fore-arm raised and slightly inclined forwards.
Finger Snapping	Snap the finger and thumb of both hands on the first beat of every bar.
Expression	Grave (i.e. not smiling). The girl is rather demure, and partners do not make a point of looking at each other while dancing, though they may do so naturally.

Dance

During the Introduction, the dancers remain motionless, standing in a natural manner, facing each other. On the last note of the Introduction a musician calls 'Primera!'.	MUSIC Bars Intro.
FIGURE I The man and woman advance towards each other in four waltz steps: short step diagonally to R, close l foot to r foot, step diagonally to R. During this step, the whole body leans slightly over to R. Repeat the waltz step	1–4 (Begin on beat 4 of bar 1)

27

CHACARERA (Chacarera del Campo)

Arranged by J. A. MORA

28

Plate 3 El Escondido.   (*Figure 6, Escondimiento-Búsqueda*)

diagonally to L, starting with the l foot, and inclining the body over to L, so that the body has a swaying movement throughout. The partners confront each other, almost touching. Still facing each other, the couple retire to their original places.

5–8

FIGURE 2: THE VUELTA

Fingers still snapping, with the same waltz step but longer paces, so that for each step the feet pass forwards, the couple follow each other round in a circle, C-C, in six waltz steps. This brings them back to their original places. The waltz step is still flat and smooth.

9–14

FIGURE 3: THE ZAPATEO-CONTORNEO

Each facing the other, in their places, the man 15–22
step dances. His arms hang loosely at his sides.
Place l foot down, flat (*four*); place r heel beside
l foot, leaning body to L (*five*); brush-beat r
foot backwards, so that r toe first hits ground
where the heel had been, and then moves back
till r toe is level with l heel (*six*).
Repeat with other foot (*one*, *two*, *three*).
Repeat r and l seven times.
Meanwhile, the woman, lightly holding her
skirt a little in front, describes a series of
small circles without turning her back on her
partner. The step is a light waltz step, very
small steps and no rise and fall.

FIGURE 4: THE VUELTA

The couple dance in a circle as in Figure 2. 23–29

FIGURE 5: THE ZAPATEO-CONTORNEO

As in Figure 3. 15–22

FIGURE 6: THE MEDIA VUELTA

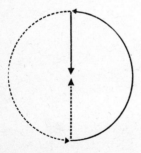

The couple begin a circle as in Figure 2, but it 23–24
ends half-way round, leaving each of them
opposite his, or her, starting point.

Now they advance towards each other, till they reach the centre, their hands almost touching the other's shoulders.

25–26

They rest thus for a moment, then withdraw, still facing each other.

27–29

Now, in the opposite places from where they started, they wait while the Introduction is played. On the last note of the Introduction, the musician cries: *Que se va la segunda!* (Let the second part go!), and the same Figures are gone through, ending with each dancer back in his, or her, original place.

El Escondido

Region	Once common all over the Republic, particularly on the pampa. Now surviving in its 'natural' state only in the north-western provinces.
Character	A dashing though dignified dance, enhanced by the pantomime incident of 'hide and seek'.
Formation	For one couple only.
Step	A flat, level waltz step, done quickly – two waltz steps to one bar of 6/8 time.
Finger Snapping	Snap the finger and thumb of both hands on the first beat of each half bar. Fingers are snapped throughout the dance, except during the pantomime (Figures 6 and 8).
Arm Position	Rather square. Upper arm almost to shoulder level, fore-arm raised and slightly inclined forwards.

Dance

The couple wait motionless, standing naturally facing each other, until Introduction is over.

MUSIC
Bars
Intro.

32

FIGURE 1: THE FIRST GIRO-ESQUINA

On the first beat of the melody, both partners move towards each other with four waltz steps, slightly diagonally to their own R, so that their l elbows almost touch. 1–2

They then spin round to their own R in three steps, r, l, r, for half a bar, and continue their progress C-C towards the next corner. 3–4

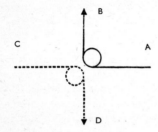

FIGURE 2: THE SECOND GIRO-ESQUINA

As in Figure 1. The partners approach each other from their new corners. 5–6

As they come abreast of each other, elbows nearly touching, they spin again and retire to new corners, still in a C-C direction. Now they are in opposite corners from where they started. 7–8

FIGURE 3: THE THIRD GIRO-ESQUINA

As before, but this time the man is on line C-D, and the woman on line A-B. 1–4

FIGURE 4: THE FOURTH GIRO-ESQUINA

As before, but this time the man is on line D-A, the woman on line B-C. Thus they end up at their starting point. 5–8

(Omit bars 9–16.)

FIGURE 5: THE VUELTA

Both dancers follow each other round in a complete circle, C-C, with sixteen waltz steps, moving forwards, and keeping at opposite sides of the circle at all points. Return to their starting point.

17–24

FIGURE 6: THE ESCONDIMIENTO-BÚSQUEDA

The woman drops on one knee (either knee), her head down a little, her hand shading her eyes to simulate hiding. The man, fingers snapping, makes a series of turns, using a flat waltz step on the spot, turning somewhat backwards on the steps as he goes round, as if seeking his partner.

9–12

He tap-dances in his place (the same zapateo step can be used as in Figure 3 of La Chacarera) making no sign, other than looking pleased, as if he has discovered her whereabouts. His arms hang loosely at his sides as he dances. The woman still kneels, as if hiding.

13–16

FIGURE 7: THE VUELTA

Exactly as in Figure 5.

17–24

FIGURE 8: THE ESCONDIMIENTO-BUSQUEDA

Exactly as in Figure 6, except that now the man 'hides' and the woman 'seeks'. She turns in her corner, fingers snapping.

9–12

Now she drops her hands, lightly holds her skirt, rather in front, and continues waltzing but in a much wider arc, with considerable élan. In doing this, she may face her partner (who is still 'hiding') all the time, or she may

13–16

ESCONDIDO

Arranged by J. A. MORA

Allegretto

(After Introductory bars, play A A, C, B, C, B, C)

turn round, as she wishes. She returns to her corner as the musical phrase ends.

FIGURE 9: THE FINAL MEDIA-VUELTA

The man and the woman follow each other round in a wide semi-circle, to finish at the other's starting point, with eight waltz steps. 17–20

When they arrive at this point, they face each other and approach with short steps, until the hands are close to the partner's hands. They stand thus until music ends. 21–24

They are now ready to repeat the whole dance from the beginning, at the end of which they will have returned to their own starting-point. On repeat of dance, the same order is kept throughout (the woman still 'hides' first time).

El Bailecito

Region   The extreme north-west of the Republic, towards the Bolivian frontier. Particularly the provinces of Jujuy and Salta.

Character   A light, quickly-moving and graceful dance.

Formation   Square dance for two couples. Shake handkerchiefs throughout Figures 1 to 4.

Step   Two waltz steps to one bar.

FIGURE 1: THE VUELTA GENERAL

Dancers stay in places. (○=woman,□=man).

MUSIC
Bars

1–4

    ○   □

    □   ○

On the fifth bar they begin dancing round in a circle, C-C, following each other, with waltz 5–15

BAILECITO (El Pajarito)

Arranged by J. A. MORA

(*Play* A, B B, A A, B)

37

steps, finishing back in their places. Men place
1 hand on belt, at the side, palm outwards.
Women with 1 hand lightly hold skirt, rather
in front. All hold a handkerchief in the air, by
one corner with r hand, and gently shake it.
(An up-and-down movement is considered
'smarter' than waving it from side to side.)

FIGURE 2: THE VUELTA DE PAREJA
Independently the couples dance, each in a
small circle, C-C, and back to their places.   5–15

FIGURE 3: THE GIROS A LA IZQUIERDA
All dancers, independently, spin (i.e. waltz   1–4
steps in tiny circle, forwards) C-C in corners.

FIGURE 4: THE GIROS A LA DERECHA
As Figure 3, but spin in opposite direction.   1–4

FIGURE 5: THE RONDA: VUELTA Y MEDIA
Each man gives a hand to each woman (still
all hold handkerchief in r hand) forming a
circle. They dance a turn-and-a-half C-C   5–15
with a lively hopping step: one foot on ground
(*one*, *two*) hop as other foot moves forward,
bending the knee and lifting foot (*three*). Set
down other foot, hop on it as first foot comes
forward. So to end.

Plate 4 *La Chacarera.* (Figure 3, *Zapateo-Contorneo*)

Bibliography

ARETZ-THIELE, Isabel. – *Música Tradicional Argentina, Tucuman, Historia y Folklore*. Universidad de Tucuman, Buenos Aires, 1946.

COLUCCIO, F. and SCHIAFFINO, G. – *Folklore y Nativismo*. Editorial Bell, Buenos Aires, 1948.

LOPEZ OSORNIO, Mario A. – *Oro Nativo*. Editorial El Ateneo. Buenos Aires, 1945.

SAUBIDET, Tito. – *Vocabulario y Refranero Criollo*. Editorial Guillermo Krafft. Buenos Aires, 1949.

VEGA, Carlos. – *Danzas y Canciones Argentinas – Teorias y Investigaciones*. Ricordi Sudamericana, Buenos Aires, 1941.

— *Las Danzas Populares Argentinas*, Vol. 1. Ministerio de Educacion, Direccion General de Cultura, Instituto de Musicologia, Buenos Aires, 1952.

— *Panorama de la Musica Popular Argentina*. Editorial Losada, Buenos Aires, 1944.